Easy

Compiled and edited by Poldi Zeitlin and David Goldberger.

Original

Piano

Duets

Music Sales America

DISTRIBUTED BY

HAL•LEONARD® CORPORATION

7777 W. BLUEMOUND RD. P.O. BOX 13819 MILWAUKEE, WI 53213

CONTENTS

Two Chorales

1

Secondo

Daniel G. Türk

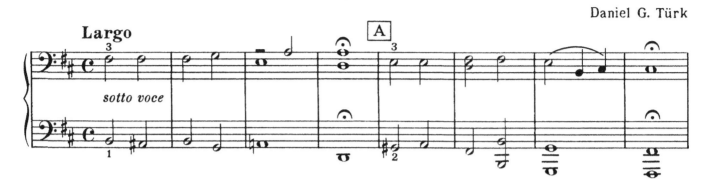

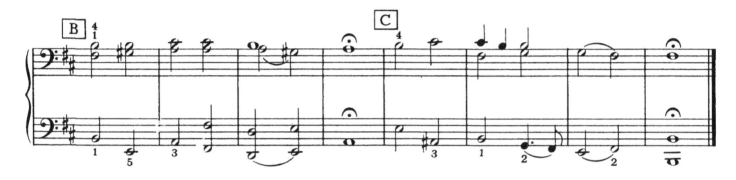

2

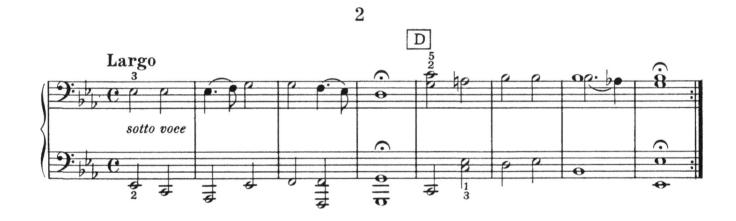

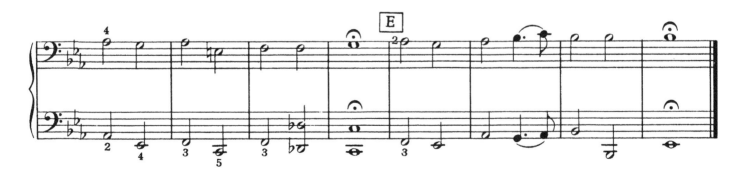

Two Chorales

1

Primo

Daniel G. Türk

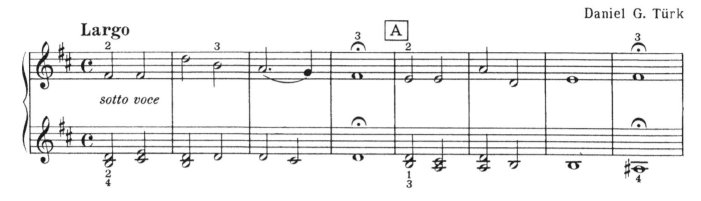

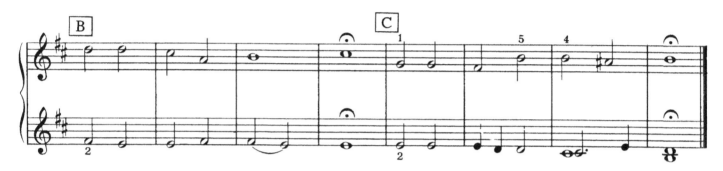

2

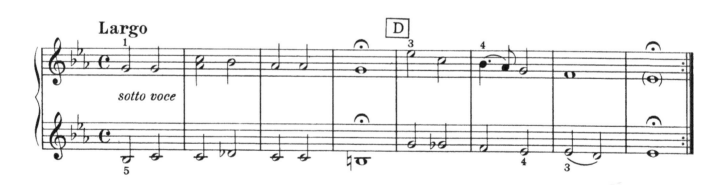

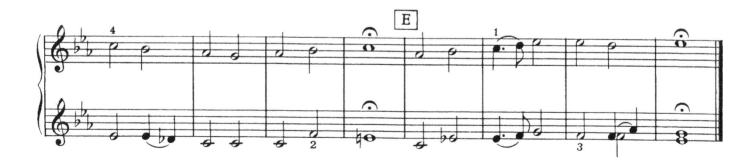

Rondo

Secondo

Daniel G. Türk

Rondo

Primo

Daniel G. Türk

The Storm

Secondo

Daniel G. Türk

The Storm

Primo

Daniel G. Türk

Allegretto grazioso All of a sudden the sky is clear

Allegretto grazioso All of a sudden the sky is clear

Finale from Sonatina

Secondo

Ernst W. Wolf

Finale from Sonatina

Primo

Ernst W. Wolf

Secondo

Primo

Minuet

Secondo

Joseph Haydn

Minuet

Primo

Joseph Haydn

Secondo

MINUET D.C. al fine

Primo

MINUET D.C. al fine

Allegro in E Minor

Secondo

Anton Diabelli

Allegro in E Minor

Primo

Anton Diabelli

Polonaise

Secondo

Anton Diabelli

Allegretto

Polonaise

Primo

Allegretto

Anton Diabelli

Hungarian Dance

Secondo

Anton Diabelli

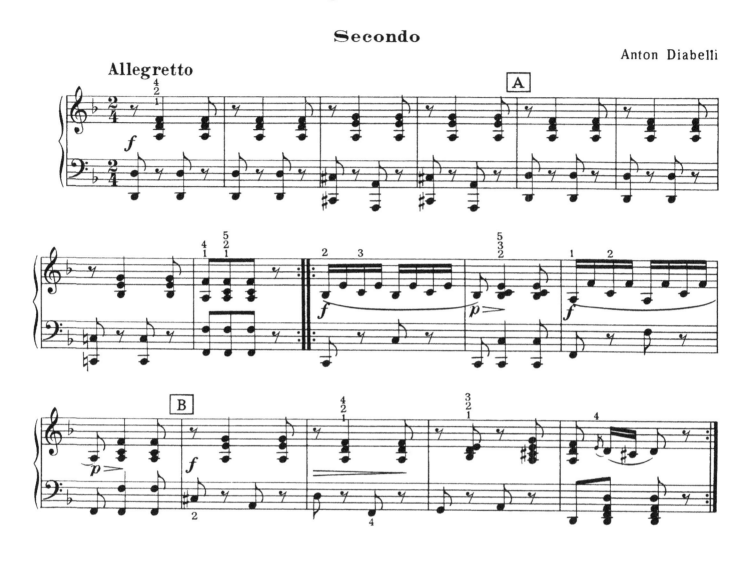

Bagatelle

Heinrich Wohlfahrt

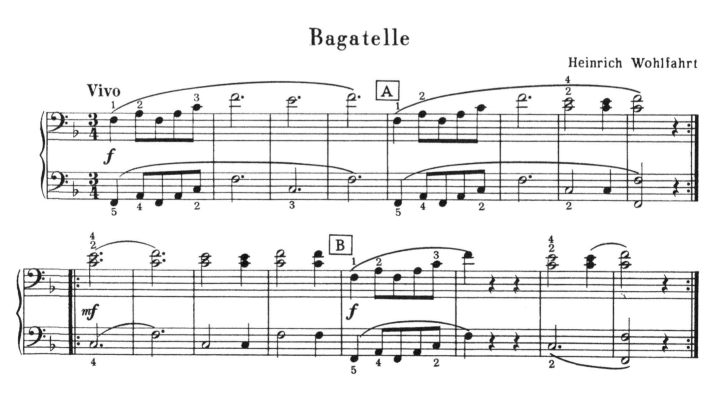

Hungarian Dance

Primo

Anton Diabelli

Bagatelle

Heinrich Wohlfahrt

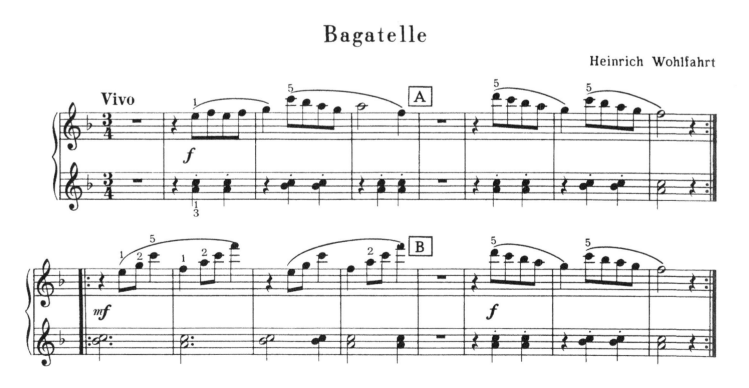

Waltz

Secondo

Heinrich Wohlfahrt

Waltz

Primo

Heinrich Wohlfahrt

Galop

Secondo

Heinrich Wohlfahrt

Galop

Primo

Heinrich Wohlfahrt

Finale from Sonata in B Flat

Secondo

Wolfgang Amadeus Mozart

Finale from Sonata in B Flat

Primo

Wolfgang Amadeus Mozart

Secondo

Two German Dances

1

Secondo

Franz Anton Hoffmeister

Two German Dances

1

Primo

Franz Anton Hoffmeister

2

Secondo

2

Primo

Gavotte

Secondo

Ludwig van Beethoven

Gavotte

Primo

Ludwig van Beethoven

Tyrolean Dance

Secondo

Karl Czerny

Melody

Karl Czerny

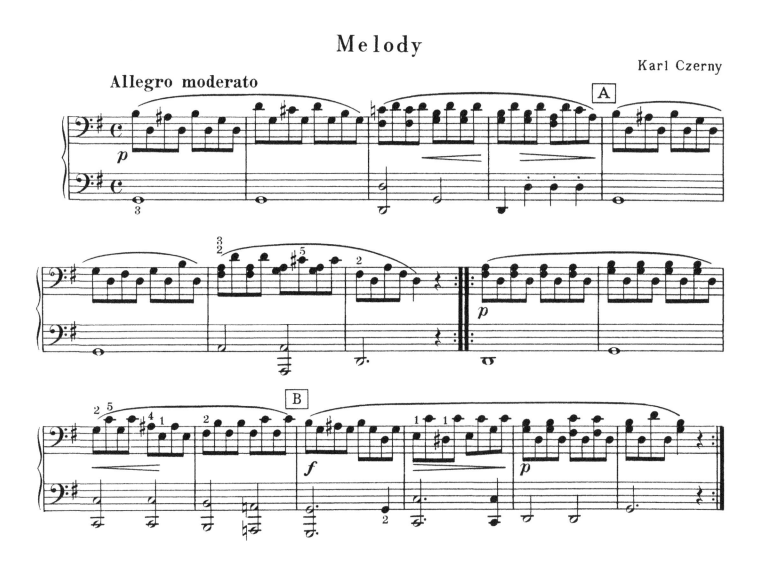

Tyrolean Dance

Primo

Karl Czerny

Melody

Karl Czerny

Andantino con Grazia

Secondo

Karl Czerny

Andantino con Grazia

Primo

Karl Czerny

Sonatina

Secondo

Carl Maria von Weber

Moderato e con amore

Sonatina

Primo

Carl Maria von Weber

Children's March

Secondo

Franz Schubert

Children's March

Primo

Franz Schubert

Secondo

D.C. al Fine

D.C. al Fine

Two Immortelles

1

Secondo

Fritz Spindler

Two Immortelles

1

Primo

2

Secondo

Fritz Spindler

2

Primo

Fritz Spindler

Secondo

Two Dances from "Quadrille"

1

Secondo

J. Friedrich Burgmüller

Two Dances from "Quadrille"

1

Primo

J. Friedrich Burgmüller

2

Secondo

Allegretto

Fine

D.C. al Fine

Primo

Allegretto

D. C. al Fine

Allegretto in C Minor

Secondo

Cornelius Gurlitt

Allegretto scherzando

Allegretto in C Minor

Primo

Cornelius Gurlitt

Allegretto scherzando

Scherzo

Secondo

Cornelius Gurlitt

Scherzo

Primo

Cornelius Gurlitt

Secondo

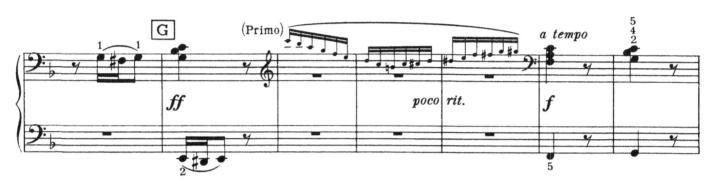

Round Dance

Secondo

Robert Schumann

Round Dance

Primo

Robert Schumann

Secondo

Secondo

poco a poco dim.

Primo

poco a poco dim.

marcato

Christmas Song

Secondo

Louis Koehler

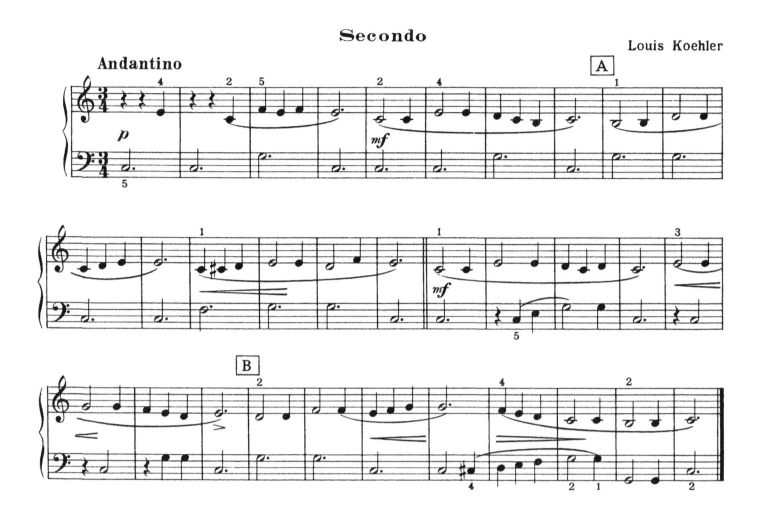

Norwegian Reindeer Song

Louis Koehler

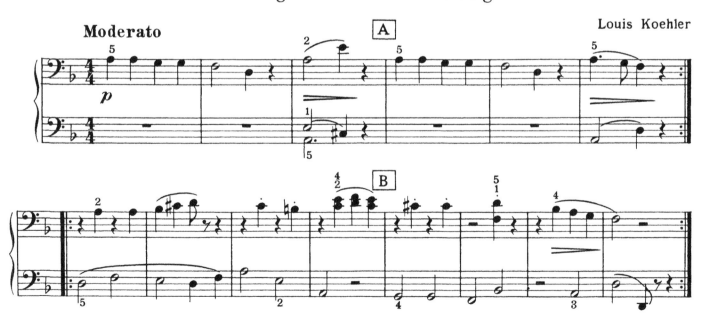

Christmas Song

Primo

Louis Koehler

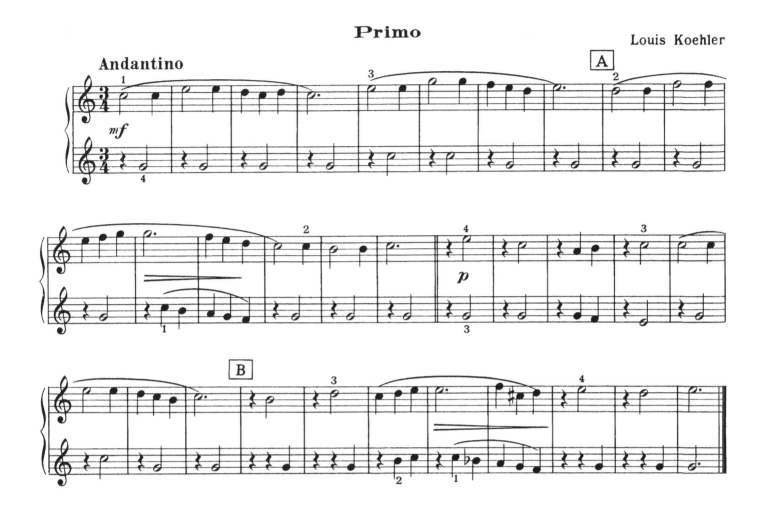

Norwegian Reindeer Song

Louis Koehler

French Folk Song

Secondo

Louis Koehler

French Folk Song

Primo

Louis Koehler

German Lullaby

Secondo

Louis Koehler

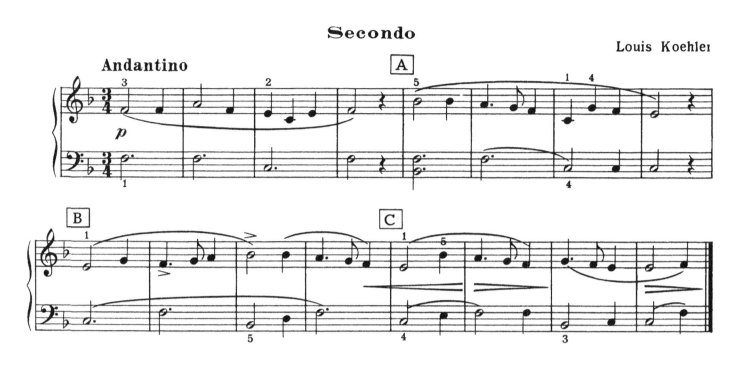

Lithuanian Song

Allegretto moderato

Louis Koehler

German Lullaby

Primo

Louis Koehler

Lithuanian Song

Louis Koehler

Tarantella

Secondo

Joseph Löw

Tarantella

Primo

Joseph Löw

Krakowiak

Secondo

Joseph Löw

D. C. al Fine

Krakowiak

Primo

Joseph Löw

D. C. al Fine

Conversation

Secondo

Heinrich Hofmann

Conversation

Primo

Heinrich Hofmann

Secondo

Ländler

Robert Volkmann

Primo

Ländler

Robert Volkmann

Moderato

Secondo

Secondo

Scherzetto

Secondo

Adolphe Blanc

Scherzetto

Primo

Adolphe Blanc

Secondo

Da Capo poi la Coda

The Lake

Secondo

Léon d'Ourville

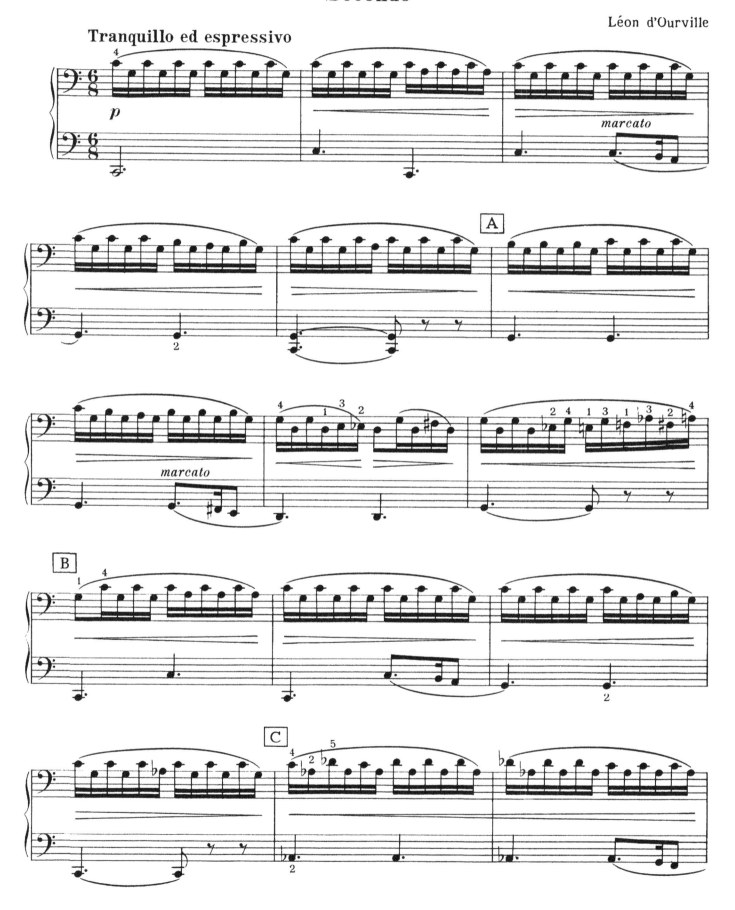

The Lake

Primo

Léon d'Ourville

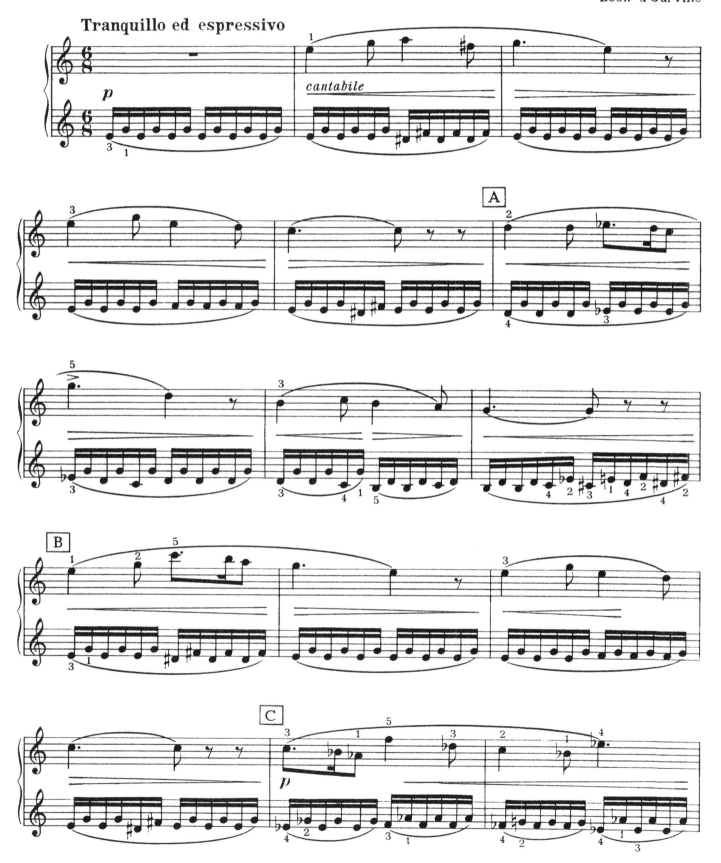

Secondo

Secondo

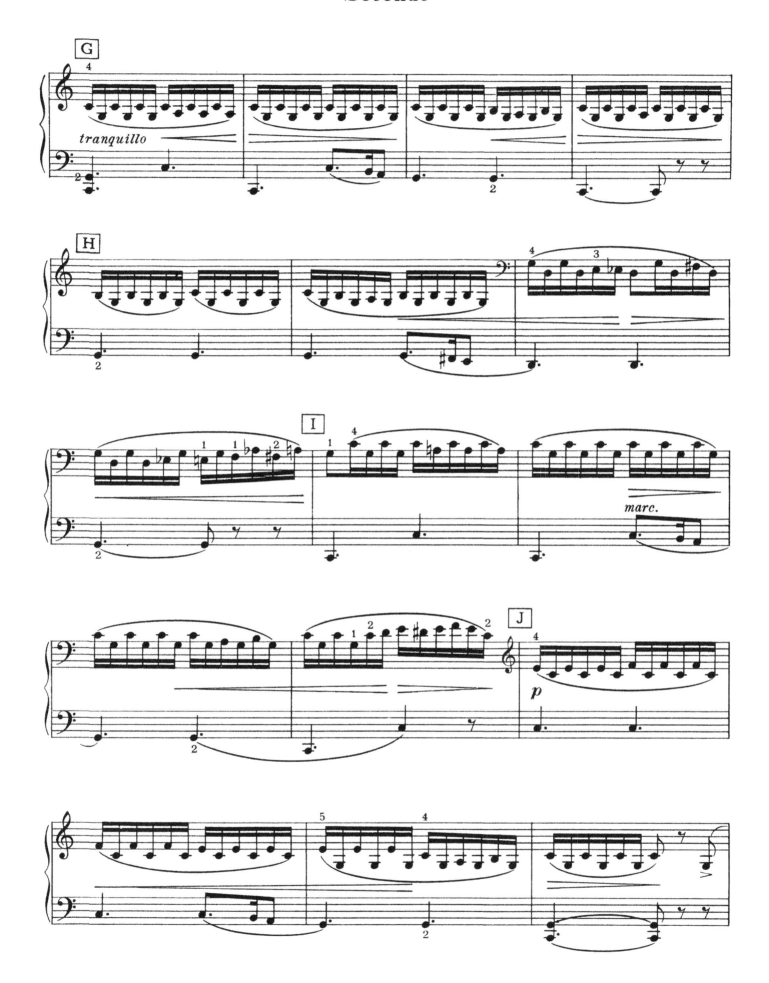

Primo

Secondo

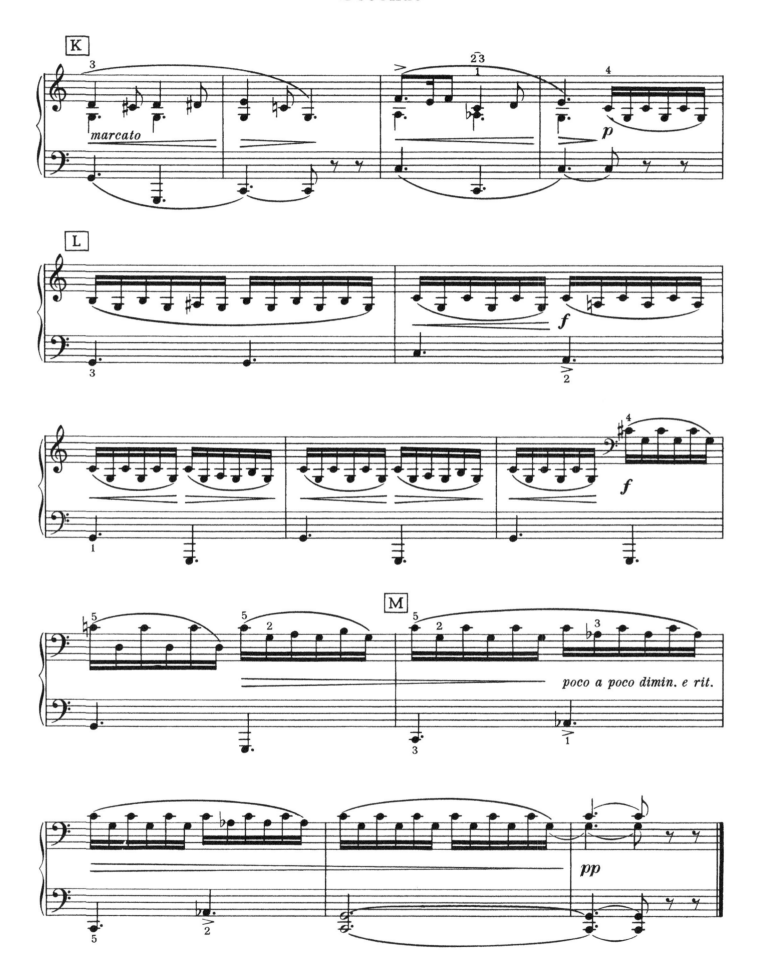

Waltz

Secondo

Johannes Brahms

Waltz

Primo

Johannes Brahms

Norwegian Dance

Secondo

Edvard Grieg

Norwegian Dance

Primo

Edvard Grieg

Allegretto tranquillo e grazioso

Secondo

Little Husband, Little Wife

Secondo

Georges Bizet

Little Husband, Little Wife

Primo

Georges Bizet

Secondo

Secondo

Little Vanya*

Peter I. Tchaikovsky

Andante

* See Primo Part

Little Vanya*

Peter I. Tchaikovsky

* Tchaikovsky used this melody in his String Quartet in D

Rustling Pine

Secondo

Peter I. Tchaikovsky

Rustling Pine

Primo

Peter I. Tchaikovsky

I Bow My Head

Secondo

Peter I. Tchaikovsky

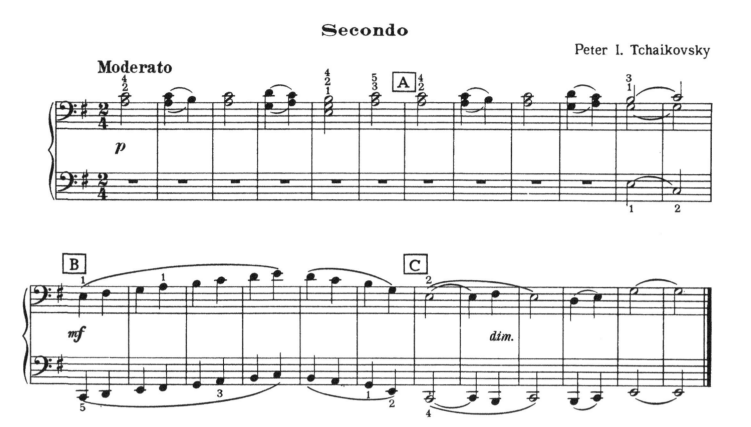

Oh, My Green Grapes

Peter I. Tchaikovsky

I Bow My Head

Primo

Peter I. Tchaikovsky

Oh, My Green Grapes

Peter I. Tchaikovsky

Sing Not, Nightingale

Secondo

Peter I. Tchaikovsky

Sing Not, Nightingale

Primo

Peter I. Tchaikovsky

On the Meadow

Secondo

Peter I. Tchaikovsky

Tears

Anton Arensky

On the Meadow

Primo

Peter I. Tchaikovsky

Tears

Anton Arensky

Secondo

The Swan

Secondo

Edward MacDowell

The Swan

Primo

Edward MacDowell

Secondo

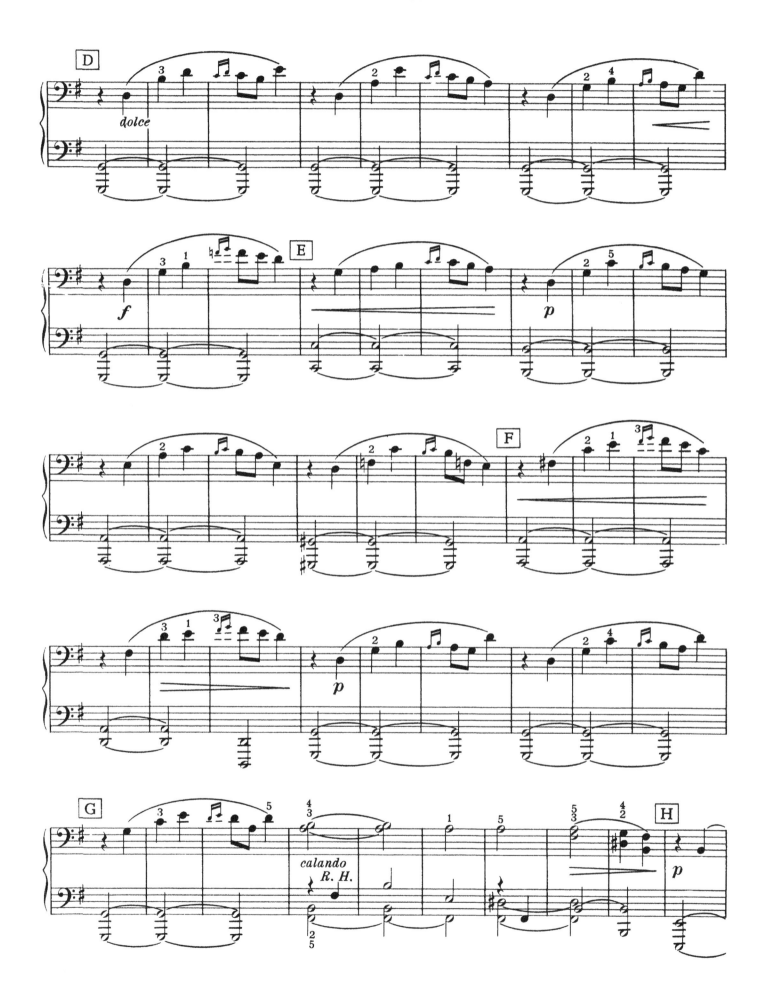

Dance of the Myosotis

Secondo

Vladimir Rebikov

Dance of the Myosotis

Primo

Vladimir Rebikov

Secondo

Three Pieces from
On the Green Meadow

1

Alexander Gretchaninoff

Secondo

Three Pieces from
On the Green Meadow

1

Alexander Gretchaninoff

Primo

2.

Secondo

2.

Primo

Secondo

3.

3.

Andante

Secondo

Igor Stravinsky

Andante

Primo

Igor Stravinsky

Polka

Secondo

Igor Stravinsky

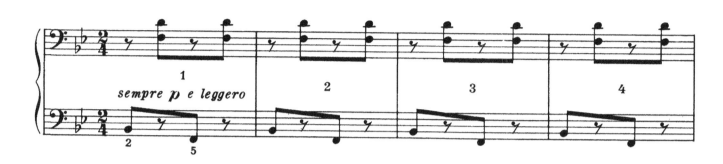

Polka

Primo

Igor Stravinsky

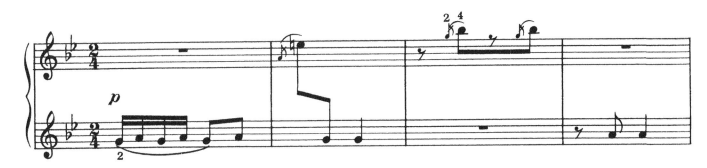

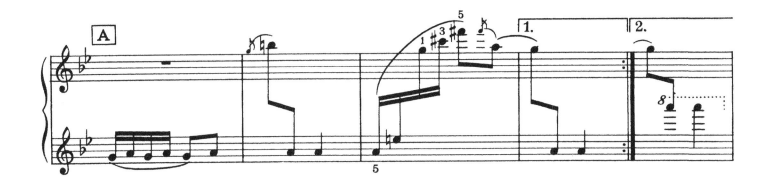

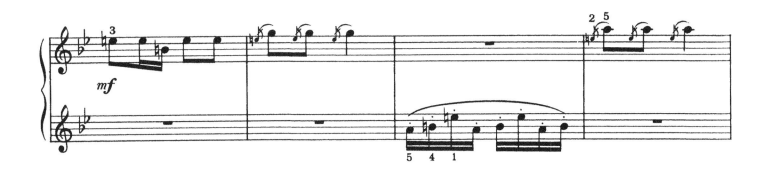

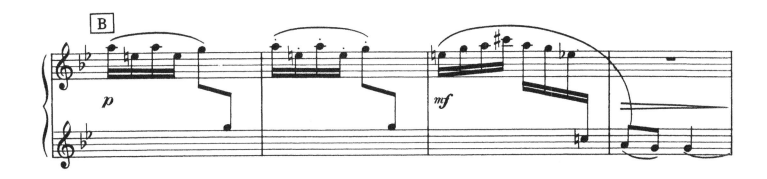

Secondo

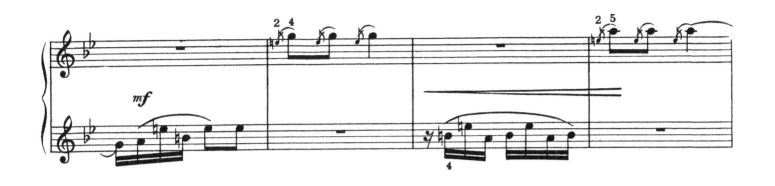

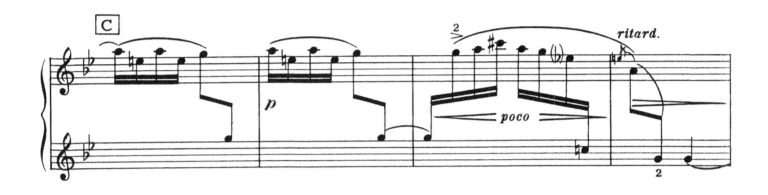

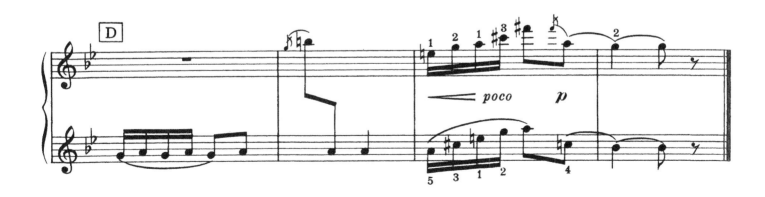